To

From

Editor: Megan Langford
Art Director: Kevin Swanson
Designer: Mark Voss
Production Designer: Bryan Ring

ISBN: 978-1-59530-295-3

BOK1161

Printed and bound in China

JUL10

GIFT BOOKS

I'll Be Me and YOU BE YOU

BY JiM HOWARD

ILLUSTRATED BY MiRNA K. STUBBS

Anna melinda
Lucinda eclair
had curly-o,
twirly-o,
girly-o hair.

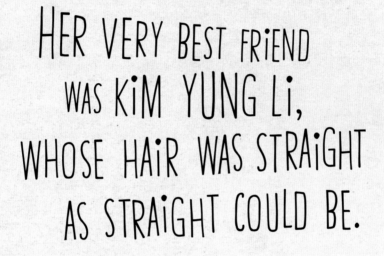

HER VERY BEST FRIEND
WAS KIM YUNG Li,
WHOSE HAIR WAS STRAIGHT
AS STRAIGHT COULD BE.

One sunny day, when Anna and Kim were hanging Like BATS from the JUNGLE GYM, Kim said to Anna,

"IF ONLY MY HEAD GREW CURLY-O, TWIRLY-O HAIR INSTEAD!"

And Anna said, "Kim, I'd trade every curl for the straight, shiny life of an untwirly girl."

And they hung by their knees and swung back and forth, one north-to-south and one south-to-north.

No one
knows how,
but the girls
bumped heads
and both yelled
"Ow!"

THEY FELL TO THE GROUND
IN A TANGLE OF HAIR
THAT WAS PART

MISS LI

AND PART

MISS ECLAIR.

THEY SAT UP AND LOOKED
AT EACH OTHER'S FACES.
SOMEHOW THEIR HAIR
HAD TRADED PLACES!

THE CURLY-O HAIR
WAS ON KIM YOUNG LI,
AND ANNA'S WAS STRAIGHT
AS STRAIGHT COULD BE!

"HOORAY!" THEY YELLED.
"WE GOT OUR WISHES!"
KIM SAID, "HAVING THESE CURLS
IS DELICIOUS."
AND ANNA, ADMIRING THE HAIR *SHE* HAD,
SAID, "SEE HOW SHINY?
I'M A SHAMPOO AD!"

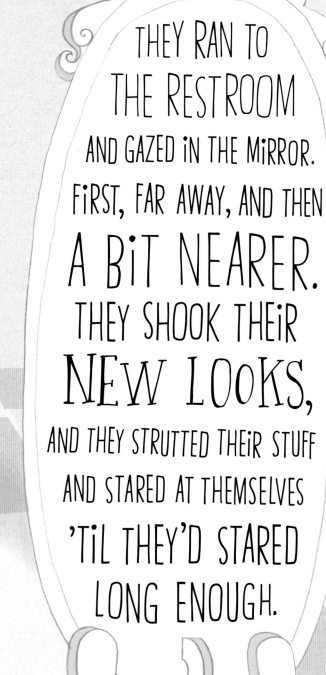

THEY RAN TO
THE RESTROOM
AND GAZED IN THE MIRROR.
FIRST, FAR AWAY, AND THEN
A BIT NEARER.
THEY SHOOK THEIR
NEW LOOKS,
AND THEY STRUTTED THEIR STUFF
AND STARED AT THEMSELVES
'TIL THEY'D STARED
LONG ENOUGH.

They saw each other and said,
"LOOK AT YOU!"
the OLD styles looked STUNNING!
BEAUTIFUL! NEW!

THEY TURNED TO EACH OTHER
AND STROKED THE HAIR
THAT HAD ONCE BEEN HERE
BUT WAS NOW OVER THERE.

Kim said, "Anna when that hair was mine,
it seemed too plain, too flat, too fine.
How I wished for curls like yours! But now...
I look at that shiny, straight hair and WOW."

And Anna said, "Kim, when I had those locks,
they seemed as pleasant as chickenpox.
It was always a problem. But now I see
that the curls on you were a cool part of me."

And somewhere in each friend's
switched-around head
grew a new idea:

BE YOURSELF INSTEAD.

"SWITCH BACK?" asked Anna.
"FOR SURE!" cried Kim.
and they ran back out
to the JUNGLE GYM.

They climbed right up,
and they hung and they swung.
They SMACKED HEADS AGAIN
and down they were flung.
The two best friends
were knocked for a loop...
Their heads were spinny,
Their BRAINS were soup!

BUT KIM WAS RE-STRAIGHTENED
AND ANNA RE-CURLED.
THEY'D RE-SWITCHEROOED
TO THEIR NORMAL-GIRL WORLD!

THEY LOOKED. AND THEY LAUGHED.
THAT WASN'T SO BAD.
THEY WERE HAPPY TO HAVE
WHAT THEY'D ALWAYS HAD.

BUT NOW KIM CAN'T SPELL.
AND ANNA CAN'T ADD.

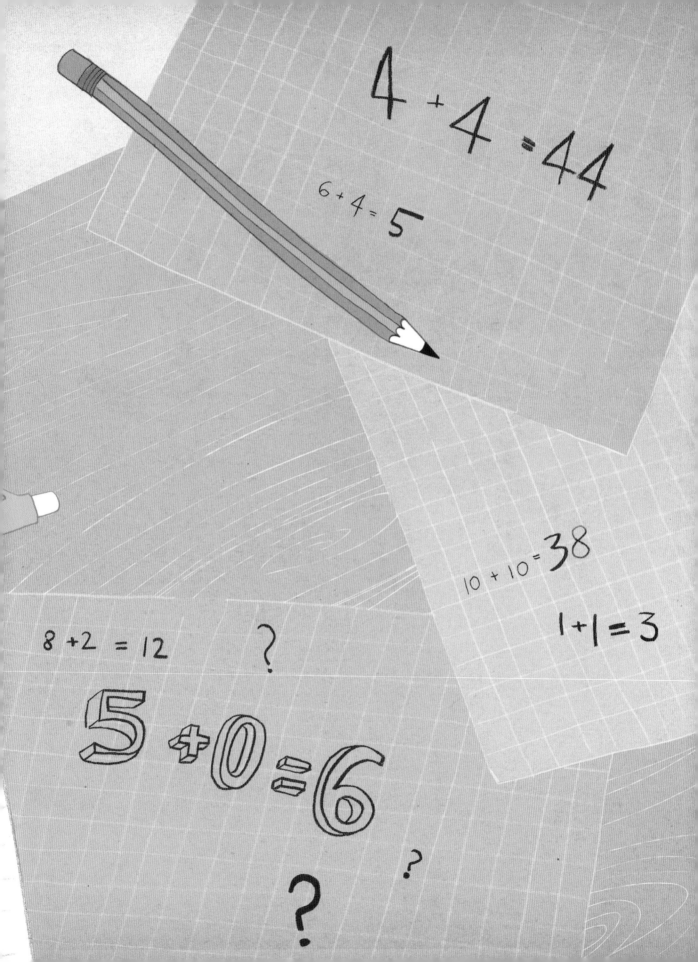

Did you like this book?
Tell us About it!

Please send your comments to:

HALLMARK BOOK FEEDBACK
P.O. BOX 419034
MAIL DROP 215
KANSAS CITY, MO 64141

OR E-MAIL US AT:
BOOKNOTES@HALLMARK.COM